Acknowled

CW00518740

All that I know is a sum total of what I have been taught, first, by the Holy Spirit, and from all those who have taught me in my journey, both directly and indirectly.

I am forever grateful to the countless exceptional people who, by their commitment and devotion to becoming the best they could be, have inspired me to do the same.

I am ever mindful of the unmatched love, prayer, support, and patience of my precious family.

To my Household of Mercy family, and the countless partners I have, who through their love and passion, tune in weekly to my online live sessions, I say THANK YOU.

CONTENTS

INTRODUCTION

The Olympics are unparalleled global sporting events. One of my favorite Olympic game is running the relay race. This is a racing competition which requires that each member of a racing team take turn completing parts of racecourse.

Interestingly, there is always someone running towards another athlete who must wait till the baton is handed over to him or her for the next lap. You must have seen athletes run with all their might just to get to the next person on the line as quickly as possible, so they can stand a better chance in the next lap.

This implies that, the athlete who runs with the baton that must be carried further will definitely influence the chances of success for the entire team. The truth is, life is a race and we are all at different spots on the race track. Therefore, the way we run our race will definitely have tremendous ripple effects and vast successive implications on the next generation.

No wonder why all we set our heart to do in life can be significantly influenced by how we start, and the help we receive at that critical point. We all need favor to start, help to continue and grace to finish the race that is set before us.

Furthermore, every building project starts with a plan. This is why, architects always provide well laid out blueprint for what we want to build. God has a blueprint and well laid out plans for our lives. Our destinies and destinations are imprints and templates of His will for us here on Earth.

As a result of this, we are spurred to learn, and understand the will of God based on His original plan for our lives, so that we will have the revelation of the big picture that He has in store for every one of us. This big picture is the blessing that flows from one generation to the next.

A blessing can be said to be some divine or supernatural aid, or reward/ a pronouncement invoking divine air, good fortune especially from one person to another or a group of people. It's important to note that blessing is always a positive pronouncement because the reverse of that is a curse.

A Generation can be defined as a body of living beings constituting a single step in the line of descent from an ancestor. So generation can always be traced back to a particular person or lineage. However, the generation could be a family (people or offspring), a nation, and land, among others.

Generational blessing is, therefore, a pronouncement invoking divine or supernatural aid, rewards or favor over a first generation or descendant to the last in space and time. It could be a divine reward transferred from one offspring to another because of sacrificial obedience towards divine instruction from God almighty. It could manifest as a result of faith or good deeds of one's ancestor. This blessing could be in the form of favor, deliverance, provision, among others.

My heartfelt desire

Unarguably, every right choice that was made by the people before us often makes it easier for us and those who come after us to ride smoothly in life. But this fact is also reflected on the opposite, if negative choices are made by those before, it becomes harder for us and the people coming after us, setting in motion hurdles to jump over and challenges to contend with before getting to breathe some fresh air, and having a fresh start.

That said, it is essential to highlight that the choices we make every day will either affect our family-line positively or negatively. In other words, living a life of distinction, honesty, help to humanity are like seeds which are planted so that our life and that of our children will be rewarding.

I want my children and grandchildren to do great things in their life because of me, not in spite of me.

I want them to ride on the back of the sacrifices and investments that I have made, things that will place them on a pedestal.

Our lives can be a stepping stone or a stumbling block. This is what differentiates generational curses from generational blessings.

The blessings supersede curses

What you continuously look at becomes magnified; Just as light is always stronger than darkness, so the blessing of God surpasses curses.

Do you believe this?

There are revelations of God imparting blessings from one generation to another. Also, the revelation of generational blessings is far more than that of generational curses. Then why do people tend to dwell on curses instead?

Well, your guess is as good as mine.

The scripture is illustrative of this. An enemy king named Balak tried to have Israel cursed by a prophet called "Balaam." After several attempts, Balaam couldn't curse the Israelites; instead, he blessed them the more; this was frustrating for Balak to handle.

Before this time, God had warned Balaam not to curse them for they were already blessed. You cannot curse what God has blessed. A curse causeless shall not come.

> *"And God said to Balaam; you shall not go with them; you shall not curse the people, for they are blessed."*

> **-Numbers 22:12**

As a believer in Christ, the same is true for us; we are already blessed because we have been identified with Jesus Christ.

And so, even if negative things have been handed down to us, God has raised us to put an end to them.

I am a partaker of the blessings

I clearly understand the power of generational blessings. I have experienced this, and I also want to teach you from God's word truth that will launch you into your lifetime of benefits, favor, and grace. So, you can pass this on to your children, grandchildren, and generation yet unborn.

This book on generational blessings emphasizes entitlements that are due us because of the work, labors, investments, or virtues of our ancestors.

Also, I want to show any person reading this book some of those entitlements, and how to get them back.

With the help of the Holy Spirit, I have written this masterpiece so that every individual, parents, and non-parents, and organizations will be empowered to release the next generation to fulfill their purpose.

To achieve this, we will take a careful look at Biblical and contemporary examples that relates the plan of God for multi-generational blessings through the family

This is not just another book to be added to your catalogue of knowledge nor your bookshelf, but one that you should read and then take conscious effort to act upon.

Enjoy this beautiful ride with me.

CHAPTER ONE

THE POWER OF GENERATIONAL BLESSINGS

"I will make you a great nation; I will bless you and make your name great, and you shall be a blessing…and in you all the families of the earth shall be blessed."

-Genesis 12:2-3

Do you know that we are blessed to be a blessing? Yes, you? It does not matter your tribe, color, background, or race; what matters is that you are connected to the grace which Christ has made available for us.

Also, the blessing of God is mighty that it can reach out to people yet unborn.

What is the blessing?

The Blessing is like an approval made on someone. It is a prayer or solemn wish imploring happiness upon another; a benediction. In other words, it is the act of pronouncing a benediction which will promote prosperity and welfare to a person.

The blessing can be spoken out, written, and passed from generation to generation.

Derek Prince defines the word Blessing as:

> *"A word spoken with some particular form of spiritual power and authority, for good or evil that sets in motion something that will probably go on from generation to generation."*

The origin of the blessing

There are several instances where the word blessing was mentioned in the Bible. The first time was in Genesis chapter 12 when God made a pronouncement directly to Abraham, with the instruction of leaving his country and the accompanying promises that followed.

> *"And I will make of you a great nation, and I will bless you and make your name great so that you will be a blessing.*
> *I will bless those who bless you, and him who dishonors you, I will curse, and in you, all the families of the earth shall be blessed."*

-Genesis 12:2-3

For the sake of clarity, it is necessary for us to also point out that though the word *'blessing'* was first used in Genesis 12, the first time a blessing was pronounced is recorded in Genesis 1:20-22, and this was not over man but on other creatures. After this instance, it was then mentioned again in Genesis 1:28 when God pronounced it over mankind.

20 And God said, Let the waters bring forth abundantly the moving creature that hath life, and fowl that may fly above the earth in the open firmament of heaven.

21 And God created great whales, and every living creature that moveth, which the waters brought forth abundantly, after their kind, and every winged fowl after his kind: and God saw that it was good.

22 And God blessed them, saying, Be fruitful, and multiply, and fill the waters in the seas, and let fowl multiply in the earth.

- Genesis 1:20-22

The difference between the 2 words, 'blessed' and 'blessing' is this.

The word *'blessed'* is the word ***'barak'*** in the original Hebrew translation and means 'To kneel; by implication to bless God as an act of adoration, or to bless man as a benefit.

Benefit as used in this context is defined as an advantage or profit gained from something. It is something intended to help.

Marriam-Webster define benefit as;
'something that produces good or helpful results or effects or that promotes well-being'

But the word *'blessing'* used in Genesis 12 is translated **'brakah'** in Hebrew. It is derived from the word blessed (barak) and means a benediction; by implication prosperity.

Check this analogy;

When you are blessed, you are a container open at the top but closed at the bottom. You allow the benefits flow into you but do not necessarily let it to flow out of the other end.

But when you are a blessing, you become a conduit for the manifestation of God's prosperity; you are not stopped at the bottom. The abundance of God flows in from one end and out on the other end.

An individual who has become a blessing is part of a linked network on both ends. These people fulfil their function and can serve God's divine purpose.

When you are a blessing, blessings don't just flow into you, they flow ***through*** you.

One sign of an individual who is a blessing is that they are always thinking of giving, seeking opportunities to give; and such people don't lack, but rather by their act of being a blessing, sets up their generations for something spectacular.

Read Provers 11:24-25 in these 2 versions;

> *24-25 It is possible to give away and become richer! It is also possible to hold on too tightly and lose everything. Yes, the liberal man shall be rich! By watering others, he waters himself*

- Proverbs 11:24-25 [Living Bible Translation]

> *24 There is the one who [generously] scatters [abroad], and yet increases all the more; And there is the one who withholds what is justly due, but it results only in want and poverty.*
> *25 The generous man [is a source of blessing and] shall be prosperous and enriched, And he who waters will himself be watered [reaping the generosity he has sown].*

- Proverbs 11:24-25 [Amplified Bible Translation]

In this first instance where the word blessing was mentioned, it can be identified that God's intention was not to leave the blessing on one man or in one generation but to pass it from one generation to the other.

Do you also realize that the blessing starts from the loins?

The Bible in Hebrews Chapter 7, verses 8 to 10 gives a picture of what a father can do to impact the lives of his children even long before they are born.

> *"Here, mortal men receive tithes, but there*
> *he receives them, of whom it is witnessed*
> *that he lives. Even Levi, who receives tithes,*
> *paid tithes through Abraham, so to speak, for*
> *he was still in the loins of his father when*
> *Melchizedek met* him."*

-Hebrew 7:8-10

The above scriptures reveal something amazing and profound. We see how Abraham paid tithes to Melchizedek, but it was the Levites that did so while still in the loins of their great-grandfather.

This tells us that, whenever we walk in the divine blessing, or God gives us something we don't deserve, we have to realize that sometimes it is because someone in our family has made some sacrifices. Anytime someone related to you does something sacrificial, they have equally set you up for success. Though to also emphasize that this does not in anyway suggest that you can obtain that blessing without aligning yourself through work and proper positioning.

It will be misleading to plant in you the idea that you can decide to be inactive, unproductive, not applying yourself resourcefully because your ancestors have made sacrifices and still expect to receive something.

Furthermore, in the eyes of God, whatever deed that a man does is very important. Do you realize that a whole generation can be cursed through alcohol, wicked imaginations, drug abuse, and immorality? So, if this can be transferred to the third and fourth generation, definitely the blessing can also be transferred from a father to other generation.

The Blessing is a covenant

The covenant that God made with Abraham tells us that, He promised to bless Abraham's seed. The term 'seed' refers to his children. More so, the evidence that a Hebrew Child has a covenant with God was the act of circumcision which was done on the eighth day after the birth of the child.

The seed (Children) are God's heritage; still, in the Bible, we see that God marks a child before they are even born. Jeremiah 1:5 explains this point. Isaac, John, Jesus, were given names before they were born.

> *"Before I formed you in the womb, I knew you; before you were born, I sanctified you; I ordained you a prophet to the nations."*

> **-Jeremiah 1:5**

The origin of our spiritual heritage began with a man who was God's friend- Abraham. At the age of seventy- five God called him out of the community he was familiar with to a land he was not familiar with. By faith, he journeyed into the unknown. At this time, he was childless, but eventually, God's promise of a child which he named Isaac came to pass.

After the death of Abraham, the Bible reveals that his son Isaac received all that Abraham had (Genesis 25:5). These included his wealth and also the covenant blessings as well. During the time of Abraham, famine struck, and he was forced to migrate to Egypt. Isaac also experienced famine and stayed back also in Egypt by the word of the Lord, and he reaped a hundred-fold during the famine (Genesis 26:12).

"And Abraham gave all that he had to Isaac."

-Genesis 25:5

"Then Isaac sowed in that land, and reaped in the same year a hundredfold, and the LORD blessed him."

-Genesis 26:12

I have seen that when we have a covenant with God, this also affect our children after us because, God is faithful. He always brings to pass whatever He has spoken. And if these children also serve God, they too will experience a higher dimension of God's blessing.

And now after Isaac

As Isaac's departure drew nigh, he spoke a blessing to Jacob unknown to him that it was his second son. The Bible states this blessing in Genesis 27:28-29.

> *"Therefore may God give you of the dew of heaven, of the fatness of the earth, and plenty of grain and wine. Let peoples serve you, and nations bow down to you. Be master over your brethren, and let your mother's sons bow down to you. Cursed is everyone who curses you, and blessed be those who bless you."*

The first son – Esau, the rightful heir, became angry on hearing that the blessing has been transferred to his brother Jacob. This made him furious and plotted to kill Jacob, but Jacob fled from his father's wealth and possession to a man named Laban. After twenty years of hard work. God blessed Jacob, and he became successful that Laban admitted this.

It is essential to underscore that the years went by, but still, it did not stop Jacob from manifesting the blessing when the time came.

You may be reading this book right now and aware of certain blessings that should have been manifest in your life as a result of the sacrifices and commitments from your ancestors. This story from Jacob is to encourage you never to give up.

> *"And Laban said to him, "Please stay if I have found favor in your eyes, for I have learned by experience that the Lord has blessed me for your sake."*

- Genesis 30:27

The confession of Laban is an exciting aspect of Genesis 30 because he openly admitted that the manifestation of his blessing was as a result of his alignment with Jacob. This is a fact that can be easily missed in this generation, as it appears, the general opinion is that the blessing only comes from those above you. In some sense, this implies to those older than you or higher in rank and position.

Another example with regards to hierarchy and the blessing is Joseph and his brothers, also, David and his brothers.

But I want to point out that Jacob already had a blessing on him, though appears to have been done just verbally, but very operational.

This highlights the fact that there are individuals and even families serving as subordinates who carry a vast amount of generational blessing on them. Such people can bring that blessing into any relationship, organization, or institution they become a part of.

Certain points illustrated in Genesis 30 for our consideration are:

➤ Jacob had a blessing already on him

➤ Jacob had not experienced the manifestation of the blessing on himself in terms of resources

➤ Laban experienced a significant increase in his business because of Jacob

➤ Jacob did not stop working for Laban, instead applied wisdom to his work

➤ And it was the last verse of the chapter that underlined Jacob's manifested blessing in terms of resources.

"And the man increased exceedingly, and had much cattle, and maidservants, and menservants, and camels, and asses."

- Genesis 30:43

Verse 43 of Genesis 30 began with a very important word, though appears insignificant – the word 'and.'

According to the dictionary, that word 'and' is used as a function word to indicate connection or addition, especially of items within the same class or type. It is used to join sentence elements of the same grammatical rank or function. It is also used as a function word to express logical modification, consequence, antithesis, or supplementary explanation.

This implies that verse 43 is directly connected to the actions of Jacob from the previous verses.

An important point to note here, especially in this generation we live in is that, working under another person, serving in another person's vision, being a significant part of another person's business and see that thing succeed, grow and increase in size can be directly connected, and have influence on what happens to your blessing becoming manifest.

Sometimes you have to serve your way to manifesting what's already on, and in you.

This does not stop here, as time went by a nation of people was birthed out of Jacob whose name was later changed to Israel. You too can plant a tree that will eventually become a legacy.

The descendants of two families were traced and here was the outcome,

Max Jukes was an atheist who married a godless woman. Some 560 descendants were traced:

Three hundred and ten died as paupers – one hundred and fifty became criminals- seven of them murderers- hundred were known to be drunkard- and more than half of the women were prostitutes.

The descendants of Max Jukes cost the U.S. government $1.25 million in the 19th-century dollars.

Jonathan Edwards was a committed Christian who gave God first place in his life. He married a godly young lady, and 1394 descendants were traced.

Two hundred and ninety-five graduated from college, of whom thirteen became college presidents and sixty-five became professors- three were elected as United States senators- three as state governors, and others were sent as ministers to foreign countries. Thirty were judges, 100 were lawyers, fifty-six practiced as physicians, seventy-five became officers in the military, hundred were well-known missionaries, preachers and prominent authors, another 80 held some form of public office, of whom three were mayors of large cities-one was the comptroller of the U.S. Treasury- and another was vice president of the United States.

All these examples show us how much power there is in generational blessings. What Legacy are you leaving for your children?

CHAPTER TWO

BLESSED TO BE A BLESSING

"When you focus on being a blessing, God makes sure that you are always blessed in abundance."

-Joel Osteen

In the previous chapter, we briefly touched on "Blessed to be a blessing," and we saw the meaning of the term 'blessing.' Here, we will delve more into what it means to be a blessing.

Light is a great influence on the environment. The presence of light dispels darkness, and it also helps its user to see clearly. If light can perform its function, how much more is a person who has been created in God's image, able to utilize the diverse features he/she has been endowed with to add value to our world?

Subsequently, an understanding of your personality, uniqueness, and identity will go a long way to help you know these features so that you can make a tremendous mark and be a blessing to others.

Mike Murdock once said that *"You will be remembered either for the problems you solve or the ones you create."*

Every day, life leaves us with a choice to either solve problems or not.

All the intelligence, ideas, wisdom, favors received, good breaks, a tender and compassionate heart, your gifting be it in administration or ministry, talents, abilities, you name it. Are they meant for you alone?

Everything that God has placed in you is not for your lifting alone; they are also meant for others. As you keep on pouring into the lives of others, God will keep blessing you the more.

Also, let us take a look at our introductory text, Genesis 12:2-3. In verse three, God told Abraham, "…and in you all the families of the earth shall be blessed." God placed the blessing of all the families of the earth in one man- Abraham. This sounds ridiculous, but that is the Almighty for you, His ways are not ours, and He has a generational approach to everything he created. This should teach us that you also have the blessing of some people inside of you.

God can be a blessing to you through anyone

The Bible in the story of 2 Kings 7 tells us an exciting story, from verse 3, four leprous men sat at the entrance of the gate reviewing their unfortunate situation. They thought to themselves if we stay here, we will die of hunger; if we move into the enemy's camp, we may be killed; which is no worse than starving.

Prior to this time, Samaria was in great famine, and under the siege of the Syrians. It was so terrible that women ate their sons as a meal for survival. At the word of the Lord through Prophet Elisha, God sent provision for this remedy, but it sounded too impossible.

In the long run, these lepers summoned courage and went into the camp. To their greatest surprise they found out that the camp was deserted because the Lord had caused the Army of the Syrians to hear the noise of the chariots and the noise of horses so, they fled in panic leaving their camp, tents, animals, food intact.

This was indeed a great celebration for the lepers. They ate and drank to their fill and took what they liked. "But they said to one another;

we are not doing right, let's go and tell others about these." Thus, the word of the Lord was fulfilled. Someone would have said "Oh, poor lepers what can they do?", But at this time, God placed the Blessing and restoration of Samaria into the hand of these people. Consequently, they became a blessing to their fellow people.

Blessed to make the name of God glorified

In 2 Corinthians 9:11, Paul told the Corinthian church, *"While you are enriched in everything for all liberality, which causes thanksgiving through us to God."*

The scripture above speaks of being enriched in "Every way." This is not limited to the area of finances but includes your field of expertise.

Therefore, whether you are an Engineer, teacher, Health care practitioner; these is not just your job, but they are platforms that God has set up for you to be a blessing. "One of the worse things we can do is to waste these opportunities."

Imagine what would have happened if Abraham had not been a blessing unto others. As God had revealed that the blessings of others were stored up on the inside of him? Or, how Laban's business would have depleted and perhaps gone into administration if Jacob had not engaged his expertise?

Therefore, channel your resources and time away from seeking your pleasure and comfort to that of people who are in dire need of them. God wants us to bless others so that His name will be shared in the world at large. Be a blessing today.

CHAPTER THREE

THE POWER OF REDEMPTION

"I will restore to you the years that the swarming locust has eaten, the hopper, the destroyer, and the cutter, my great army, which I sent among you."

-Joel 2:25

The restoration of generational blessings is something that is very strong on my heart, because I have over time seen how people have been deprived from blessings that their parents and ancestors laboured for. Blessings that they should have walked into by heritage. This can affect cities, communities and even countries, but is not often emphasised.

What are the things you have identified that your ancestors laboured for, things that should have added to you, advanced your life, reduced your present pain, choreographed your life for a performance that would have positively impacted your generation and those after?

As a leader of a family, organisation and even a nation, have you identified blessings that is due you and your people because of the sacrifices of generations before yours.

I believe that a tribe or community can lay claim to the blessings that their ancestors laboured for.

There are some seeds that you have sown that you may not reap the harvest, but God has designed them for your children or your grandchildren. Likewise, you didn't get to where you are on your own; somebody prayed, sowed seeds of kindness, made sacrifices on your behalf to make you arrive where you are today.

More so, some blessings were not accrued to your parents or grandparents even though they were entitled to get them. You can call them back to you. This is what is called the power of Redemption.

> *"You know, there are in many lives, there are families where, maybe not you, but maybe your grandparents, your great-grandparents had something stolen from them. Do you know you can spiritually and legally call that back to you?"*

- Sid Roth (Its Supernatural Network)

The act of getting back is called 'The power of Redemption.'

And redemption means that which was lost is reclaimed and brought back in.

In the Old Covenant, what Adam lost in the garden was restored by Jesus through the New Covenant; the resurrection has restored us into that place where we can recover all of those things.

When we talk about Restore or getting it back, we are reminded of the prophecy in Joel which says:

> *"I will restore to you the years that the swarming locust has eaten, the hopper, the destroyer, and the cutter, my great army, which I sent among you."*

-Joel 2:25

Taking close attention to the verse above, we will discover that the years, as mentioned in there is the past that has been lost or wasted.

What most people do not seem to realize is that there are blessings that are due us because of our ancestors, but instead we have often focused on the curses we inherited because of their sins, and not take back what is rightfully ours, maybe because we do not know.

So, we suffer, stay in lack, live from hand to mouth, and lead a very mediocre life because of our lack of knowledge.

Identification of generational blessings

Knowing or identifying what is yours is very instrumental in making necessary steps to getting it. We are reminded of the statement in the book of Hosea;

> *"My people are destroyed for lack of knowledge."*

> **-Hosea 4:6a**

It is essential that we seek knowledge because it is the only way out of misery and ignorance

Let us take a close look at the below verses in 2 Samuel 9: 1-13

> *"And David said, "Is there still anyone left of the house of Saul, that I may show him kindness for Jonathan's sake?"*
> *2 Now there was a servant of the house of Saul whose name was Ziba, and they called him*

to David. And the king said to him, "Are you Ziba?" And he said, "I am your servant."

3 And the king said, "Is there not still someone of the house of Saul, that I may show the kindness of God to him?" Ziba said to the king, "There is still a son of Jonathan; he is crippled in his feet."

4 The king said to him, "Where is he?" And Ziba said to the king, "He is in the house of Machir, the son of Ammiel, at Lo-debar."

5 Then King David sent and brought him from the house of Machir, the son of Ammiel, at Lo-debar.

6 And Mephibosheth, the son of Jonathan, son of Saul, came to David and fell on his face and paid homage. And David said, "Mephibosheth!" And he answered, "Behold, I am your servant."

7 And David said to him, "Do not fear, for I will show you kindness for the sake of your father Jonathan, and I will restore to you all the land of Saul, your father, and you shall eat at my table always."

8 And he paid homage and said, "What is your servant, that you should show regard for a dead dog such as I?"

9 Then the king called Ziba, Saul's servant,
and said to him, "All that belonged to
Saul and all his house I have given to your
master's grandson.

10 And you and your sons and your servants
shall till the land for him and shall bring in the
produce that your master's grandson may have
bread to eat. But Mephibosheth your master's
grandson shall always eat at my table." Now
Ziba had fifteen sons and twenty servants.

11 Then Ziba said to the king, "According to all
that, my lord, the king commands his servant, so
will your servant do." So Mephibosheth ate at
David's[a] table, like one of the king's sons.

12 And Mephibosheth's had a young son, whose
name was Mica. And all who lived in Ziba's
house became Mephibosheth's servants.

13 So Mephibosheth lived in Jerusalem, for he
always ate at the king's table. Now he was lame
in both his feet.

Our text begins with a very simple word with
so much significance; *'and.'* The word *'and'*
when used to introduce a sentence, implies
continuation, which suggests to me that the
request made by King David about his desire
to release generational blessings was not
made out of boredom nor compulsion, but by

divine prompting. There was a divine push from heaven.

Also, the scriptures in Esther 6:1-3 reminds us of this fact regarding king Xerxes and Mordecai:

> *"On that night, the king could not sleep. And he gave orders to bring the book of memorable deeds, the chronicles, and they were read before the king. And it was found written how Mordecai had told about Bigthana and Teresh, two of the king's eunuchs, who guarded the threshold, and who had sought to lay hands on King Ahasuerus. And the king said, "What honor or distinction has been bestowed on Mordecai for this?" The king's young men who attended to him said, "Nothing has been done for him."*

We read of no illness that broke the king's sleep, but God, who gives the gift of sleep to His beloved, withheld it from him.

This scripture reveals that Ahasuerus was:

➤ A powerful king.

➤ A king with so much influence,

➤ A king, who commanded 127 provinces, could not command one hour's sleep.

Look at the steps that Jehovah took towards the advancement of Mordecai. The king could not sleep when Jehovah had a design to serve in keeping him awake.

It doesn't matter how people pretend to be the controlling factor in your life and destiny. It doesn't matter how they threaten to open or shut any doors for you. You should never be afraid because, Esther 6 that we just read proves to us that God's sovereign hand controls all events.

Psalm 47:8 explains;

"God sits on His throne and rules over the nations" - *this means our God, Jehovah is in charge.*

Back to our story:

One of the interesting points to note is that King David in the preceding chapter had just returned from series of wars and battles, so it amazes me how he can switch from conquering and capturing to a calculated and coordinated move in releasing generational Blessings.

This brings me to the point that when the set time comes for God to release blessings that are due you as a result of the sacrifices and investment made by your ancestors, it doesn't matter what mood or state of the economy, the people in position are, He activates them into action with you on their mind.

Nothing can stop your restoration

When the time comes for God to restore to you the years that the locust, cankerworm, caterpillar, and palmerworm have eaten,

When the time comes for God to restore to you, blessings that your ancestors were cheated from, it doesn't matter what controversial or conflicting situation is happening around the people in authority at that time; He will activate them into remembering you and what is due you.

This, therefore, throws some light on Proverbs 21:1 which reads;

> *"The king's heart is like a stream of water directed by the Lord; he guides it wherever he pleases."*

That is to say; it is only God that can direct the heart of anyone, including the King as He pleases, most especially for His purposes and will to come into existence.

Henceforth, never feel sorry for yourself, because there are people whose promotion is indirectly connected to your liberation.

There are people stepping up to occupy positions because of your possession.

There are people advancing professionally because of the release of your properties.

Some laws and policies are amended because of you.

Declarations:

Father, thank you for the favor I have before you and man.

I declare that people go out of their way to bless me and to help me because of the generational blessings that are operational in my life.

I have favor with everyone that I deal with and come into contact with today. Doors that were once closed are now opened for me.

I receive preferential treatment, and I have special privileges as a result of the blessings inherited from my ancestors. I declare that I am God's favored child.

Mephibosheth

The story of Mephibosheth can be hard to comprehend and fathom, but when it comes to God, there is no situation that He cannot change. He is always working wonders in secret places.

Taking a look at how King David enquired about the house of Saul in verse 3 of 2 Kings 9 suggest to me that, except a divine influence comes upon people in authority, their hearts will not be stirred towards you.

In 2 Kings 9:3, Ziba described that Mephibosheth was lame at both feet; he was limited and invalid.

It is common for people to name you after your shortcomings. They seem to think that giving a vivid description of your limitation, weaknesses, and challenges would eliminate you from the selection process, but what they fail to understand is that this Blessing is not coming on you because of you.

What you and the people around do not seem to understand is the fact that the next blessing that manifests in your life has nothing to do with your sacrifices. Which means, their visual analysis of your seeming insignificance and past failures cannot stop it from manifesting.

His response in verse eight reveals that even Mephibosheth didn't count himself as anyone that deserves mercy.

God can make a pauper become a prince in one moment, all of a sudden; you will have an enterprise working for you by one prophetic instruction.

Take a moment and make this declaration several times until it sinks in;

'I am significant, productive, powerful and relevant because of the blessing on my life as a child of the king — Jehovah'

It does not matter where you are right now, but there are people that God has stirred up to set up things for you, the blessing that is coming for you. This may be something that you didn't work, pray, shout, fast, nor labor for.

Who was Ziba?

The second verse in our text introduces a man named Ziba. He was a man who had served under the authority of Saul. He was a person who became instrumental in identifying and introducing Mephibosheth to the king for the singular purpose of receiving his generational blessing. This man Ziba is very strategic in the entire process of restoring the blessings on Mephibosheth.

But let us first establish some facts about this man:

The name 'Ziba' in the original Hebrew translation meaning 'To station.' The word station comes from the Latin word 'stationem' for 'a job or position,' through the word 'stare' which means 'to stand.'

A station is a place or building where a specified activity or service is based. Therefore, to station, someone is to put or assign the person to a specified place for a particular purpose, especially in the military aspect.

Ziba had twenty servants with a large family containing fifteen children; this shows that he was comfortable. He was not just any type of servant.

This reinforces my understanding that God strategically stations or position people that will connect and reconcile you to every blessing that is due you.

Let us make another declaration because the words in our mouths are powerful:

"I declare that the people responsible to reconcile me to every blessing due me has been strategically positioned.

I also declare that they will find me through Jehovah's influence."

Your blessings await you

Taking a look at the significance of a generational blessing, there are people whom God has assigned to places, given notable position, trained in particular areas, skilled in unique things just because of the responsibility to ensure that you are linked to what is due you.

This may be very challenging to contain, but people are ascending some levels in a certain organization and even in government who are given such access with you in mind.

Certain political positions have been occupied because policies that will proceed, bills that will be sponsored out of that office will change the course of your life for good.

Consequently, some people have won an election in a particular constituency by a very small margin, just because they have been divinely assigned a very important task of ensuring that you are aligned with generational blessings due you, and you don't even know it.

During one of our online live prayer meetings, I mentioned that certain generational blessings were stolen from your family, which will be restored. Some people have identified these stolen blessings and are expecting the restoration to come from the people that stole it. God has initiated a process of recovery just like was declared in Joel 2, but the only difference is that it will come through an avenue you never imagined.

I believe that the magnitude of generational blessing due you is beyond the people who stole it initially. So, God will orchestrate a situation that will facilitate the release of that blessing from a source unexpected.

For some people, the individuals or families who stole what belong to you may have all passed away, but this does not negate the fact that something was stolen from you.

God in His infinite mercies has positioned a person or an institution that will make restoration possible for you.

As we conclude this chapter, one question we must ask ourselves is;

Am I making life more comfortable or more difficult for the generations coming after me?

Can my faithfulness and service to God and humanity extend to the fourth generation?

We must live our lives in a way that will cause the people coming after us to win.

Say these prayers with faith.

- My father God, I pray that you strategically position everyone who has a link to the place of influence that involves my generational blessings. And Lord, I ask that you cause them to find me in due time.

- I declare in prayer that God has stirred the hearts of the people in authority and position towards me, people who have the power to release every blessing that is due me because of the sacrifices made by my ancestors.

- I declare that some very powerful people are losing sleep to do me good

- I declare that serious deliberations are taking place to favor me

- I declare that an impromptu committee has been formed, set up, and commissioned to work on strategies and plans that are favorable to me.

- According to Deuteronomy 1:11, I declare that I have wisdom beyond my years and that I accomplish dreams that did not originate with me, in Jesus name. Amen.

CHAPTER FOUR

BEFORE YOU DEPART, IMPART IT!

"A righteous man will leave an inheritance for his children's children..."

-Proverbs 13:22

When we soberly reflect over the unavoidable realities of life and death; we are left with several questions. Most of these questions are bordered around the eternal value of our words and deeds in this world.

This chapter has been thoughtfully included to challenge you to think carefully about the legacy you are leaving behind for the next generation. This goes beyond your houses, cars, businesses, wealth, and position going by the world's standard. Are you a blessing to the next generation? What would you be remembered for? Why should people rejoice over the life you are living right now? Would the next generation be better off because of you or struggle to prosper in spite of you? Think about these things?

The Bible is filled with men and women who stood as the channels of generational blessings for people who came after them. God has over the years been particular about looking for a man whom He can work with to bring to pass His blessing and counsel to successive generations of people on Earth.

The power of one man or woman

You see, numbers do not limit God. In fact, whenever God wants to wrought deliverance for a generation, He is not always particular about multitudes. Most times, He will partner with just one man or woman through whom blessings and deliverance will be released to countless millions without limitations of time and distance. In this chapter we shall see a few Biblical examples of men and women who God used mightily to perpetuate blessings from one generation to another.

1. Consider Abraham.

> *"That in blessing I will bless thee, and in multiplying I will multiply thy seed as the stars of the heaven, and as the sand which is upon the sea shore; and thy seed shall possess the gate*

of his enemies; and in thy seed shall all the
nations of the earth be blessed; because thou hast
obeyed my voice."

-Genesis 22:17-18

Abraham was a man of far-reaching impact and undying influence over several cultures, religion, and races of the Earth even after departing the earth many years ago. Believers everywhere still invoke and associate with the blessing of God that was upon Abraham. I remember singing in Sunday school while growing up that we are children of Abraham and therefore partaker of the blessing. What a glorious life!

This is a typical example of generational influence. Today, many wealthy people only amass wealth that does not exceed the immediate generation after them.

However, due to a close walk with God, Abraham received abundant and countless blessings. God said to Abraham: "In blessing, I will bless you...!" In other words, I am going to release a dimension of blessing to you that is second to none; so great an achievement for most people, when you become listed as one of the wealthiest men in the planet. But Abraham also secured a blessing even for generations unborn. God said in Him shall all the families of the earth draw their blessing. That is amazing! So the blessing released on Abraham did not end in the generation after him, but God has all the families of the earth in view while releasing the blessing.

You may ask that I wasn't born in his days and am not from Israel, my family is totally far from Israel, so how then is my family connected to this blessing?

> *"And if ye be Christ's, then are ye Abraham's seed, and heirs according to the promise."*

> **-Galatians 3:29**

Every child of God that believes in Christ has automatically become the seed of Abraham regardless of where you were born or your race and tribe. The Bible also says that we are partakers of the blessing that was upon Abraham. So take your eyes off the condition of your family if it's not enviable and connect to the Abrahamic generational blessing. More discussion about Abraham will be unveiled in the next chapter.

2. David

*"The scepter shall not depart from Judah, nor
a lawgiver from between his feet, until Shiloh
come; and unto him shall the gathering of
the people be."*

-Genesis 49:10

This verse shows the proclamation of God upon
the tribe of Judah. Out of all the children of
Israel, the scepter, which signifies the throne,
will not depart from the lineage. It means
anyone that will be king over all the other
eleven tribes must be from Judah. Interestingly,
at the time this was declared, there was no
thought that one day, the children of Israel will
be in need of a king. As a matter of fact, they
have not even gotten to the period where Judges
led them. But Judah has secured the throne for
his generation till eternity.

When David finally became a king who also
was from the tribe of Judah, God made another
declaration of generational blessing upon him in
1 Kings 2:4;

*"That the LORD may continue his word which
he spake concerning me, saying, If thy children*

*take heed to their way, to walk before me in
truth with all their heart and with all their soul,
there shall not fail thee (said he) a man on the
throne of Israel."*

God promised David that there will always
be a man on the throne among his children.
So David further secured the throne for his
generation yet unborn which began from
Solomon. So Solomon became king over Israel
by virtue of the generational blessing from God
upon the lineage of Judah. If for any reason
Solomon was born to a different tribe, he likely
Would have missed out in succeeding David as
king. So, we see again the effect of the blessings
of the Lord upon a man reflecting in the life of
many other people even after the demise of the
original carrier of the blessing. The good news
is Jesus is the king of kings, and He is also from
the tribe of Judah. So you can see that you can
live a life today that settles your entire lineage
from generation to generation.

3. **Esther**

The story of Esther remains relevant even in our
days. Esther was an orphan who was brought
up by her uncle. We can suppose that she never

really had the best of education and upbringing that everyone will possibly look out for. Yet she became a major instrument for the deliverance of an entire race. A decree was made by the king which was masterminded by Haman in Esther 3:13;

> *"And the letters were sent by posts into all the king's provinces, to destroy, to kill, and to cause to perish, all Jews, both young and old, little children and women, in one day, even upon the thirteenth day of the twelfth month, which is the month Adar, and to take the spoil of them for a prey."*

The decree was to destroy all the Jews in the land from the youngest to the eldest, male and female. Haman had all the power and resources to execute that plan. But then Esther stood in the gap for the Jews. She called for a fast before she broke the protocol to appear before the king, which could lead to her death, because no one appears before the king except he sends for the person. She found favor in the sight of the King, and the Jews were spared while Haman and his household died. Esther became a channel that God used to initiate generational deliverance to the Jews, if not they could have been wiped out of the land, and their race would probably have been terminated. She sacrificed her life and was ready to die to save the Jews.

4. Lois

Generational blessing is not just in terms of money or possessions but also in faith. This could be the most important generational impact ever. We are Christians today because the faith in Jesus was securely passed on to us from generation to generation.

> *"When I call to remembrance the unfeigned faith that is in thee, which dwelt first in thy grandmother Lois, and thy mother Eunice; and I am persuaded that in thee also."*
>
> **-2Timothy 1:5**

From the verse above, Lois is the grandmother of Timothy. Not much was about her and her exploits while on earth, but one most important significance of that special life is about her faith. The Bible described her faith as genuine, which means sincere and un-hypocritical. She walked with God In such a way that aside many other unnamed generational blessings that flowed from her this unfeigned faith was evident in her protégé. The same was recognized in Eunice and eventually in Timothy who later became a Bishop through the laying on of hands by Apostle Paul. So we saw a generation that bears the sincere unalloyed faith. The stability and steadfastness of Timothy and his relevance in the churches planted by Paul can be traced back to the generation he belonged to.

5. Mary (The mother of Jesus)

"And, behold, thou shalt conceive in thy womb and bring forth a son, and shalt call his name JESUS.
He shall be great, and shall be called the Son of the Highest: and the Lord God shall give unto him the throne of his father, David:
And he shall reign over the house of Jacob forever, and of his kingdom, there shall be no end."

-Luke 1:31-33

The deliverance of every generation always begins with a man. When God was about to start the actualization of the redemption of man, it all began with the birth of the Messiah, and Mary was found worthy for the assignment.

Her ability to bring up the Messiah correctly is needed, because the redemption of the world is connected to the birth of the messiah. Till date, the world still celebrates the impact of Mary in the redemption of the world.

6. Jesus

"Saying with a loud voice, worthy is the Lamb that was slain to receive power, and riches, and wisdom, and strength, and honor, and glory, and blessing

-Revelation 5:12

History tells us that Jesus lived for over thirty years, and the world is yet to recover from life and sacrifice from Jesus. He had rough background and birth, but that did not deter His impact on the earth. A meaningful life is possible around the world today by the death of Jesus, which was significant to the redemption of the man. Through His death, we are delivered from poverty to riches and blessing, from shame to glory, from foolishness to wisdom, from weakness to strength, from darkness to light, from death to everlasting life. He came to reconcile us back to God, making us children of

God. His life, teachings, and ministry remain the pattern of life for all Christians worldwide to date. The dominion of man that was lost to the devil in the Garden of Eden was recovered by the effect of the life of Jesus going from generation to generation.

CHAPTER FIVE

ABRAHAM'S BLESSINGS ARE MINE

"Now the LORD had said unto Abram, Get thee out of thy country, and from thy kindred, and from thy father's house, unto a land that I will shew thee: So Abram departed, as the LORD had spoken unto him…"

-Genesis 12:1, 4

Abraham remains a good example of an all-time generational blessing personified, but this did not come by mere wishes or prayers, but by complete obedience to instructions which God gave him. At different times, God gave Abraham various instructions which he obeyed. Let's take a glance at some of the instructions of God that Abraham obeyed;

- **The call from his father's house**

Abraham started his work with God on a frequency of dictate. At first, God's appearance to him was a demand to follow instruction. He promised to bless him and in turn, bless all that blesses him yet assuring that anyone who curses him is cursed, but all this will only happen because Abraham departed. Failure to depart from his father's house may have exempted him from the blessing which was beyond him.

A PEEP INTO A LIFE OF SACRIFICE

"Come to me my people who have made a covenant with me by sacrifice."

-Psalm 50:5

It is necessary for us to understand that the sacrifices of today are the platforms and seeds of blessings for generations to come. Abraham was an epitome of sacrificial living and giving in almost every ramifications and season of his life. His lifestyle is truly a challenge for you and I to adopt.

- **What is your "Isaac"?**

  "And it came to pass after these things that God did tempt Abraham, and said unto him, Abraham: and he said, Behold, here I am. And he said, Take now thy son, thine only son Isaac, whom thou lovest, and get thee into the land of Moriah; and offer him there for a burnt

offering upon one of the mountains
which I will tell thee of.
And Abraham rose up early in the morning, and
saddled his ass, and took two of his young men
with him, and Isaac his son, and clave the wood
for the burnt offering, and rose up, and went
unto the place of which God had told him."

- Genesis 22:1-3

This seems to be the most remarkable event of all which God commanded Abraham to do that made him a reference point for a generational blessing. After waiting for his covenant child for twenty-five years, God put him in a situation that required him to sacrifice the child he waited all those years to receive even though there were several animals that could be used as sacrifice, yet Abraham woke up the next day and moved to obey God. As he attempted to sacrifice his son, God stopped him and unleashed a generational blessing on him.

Certainly, one effective way to connect to generational order of blessing is through the covenant of giving. Abraham was ready to give his only son as a sacrifice to secure that blessing.

Jesus gave His life to redeem humanity from their sin and secured that generational blessing.

Abraham obeyed God, and a generational blessing was released on him, but for you to benefit from this blessing, Jesus said you must also do likewise; obeying God just like Abraham did is the way to connect to the blessing instead of doing whatever pleases you and following your own pattern.

> *"They answered and said unto him, Abraham is our father. Jesus saith unto them, If ye were Abraham's children, ye would do the works of Abraham."*

- John 8:39

David is not left out

We also see that David secured blessings of been on the throne for his generation. God was set to continue the race as long as His instructions were obeyed. The throne will remain in the house of David forever simply by obeying God and walking in His precepts.

> *"That the LORD may continue His word which He spake concerning me, saying, If thy*

*children take heed to their way, to walk before
me in truth with all their heart and with all
their soul, there shall not fail thee (said he) a
man on the throne of Israel."*

- 1Kings 2:4

Have you considered sacrificial living?

The life you live today will either secure the
future for your seed or destroy it. Ponder on this.
Many people are suffering and going through
some hardship today due to the selfish choices
made by the people ahead of them. Daniel and
the three Hebrew boys were taken into captivity
in Babylon not because of what they did wrong
but due to a step taken by their ancestor, which
became a painful experience for them.

*'And when Abram was ninety years old and
nine, the LORD appeared to Abram and said
unto him, I am the Almighty God; walk before
me, and be thou perfect."*

- Genesis 17:1

Daniel began his walk in the land of captivity
by consecrating himself to God, he purposed
never to eat of the King's meat nor defile

himself. This secured a perfect walk with God in the land of Babylon where he was justified to misbehave. By this act, God revealed the happenings in the future to him and the time they were supposed to be in captivity.

This highlights the fact that you cannot please God in sin or unrighteousness. Nobody is acceptable before God while dwelling in sin. Only the son is entitled to the inheritance of the house, the blessing is for members of the household, and one way to become the son of God is by salvation, therefore, consecrate yourself to God then you'll become an heir to the promise.

Full length and not Partial obedience

"This is my covenant, which ye shall keep, between you and me and thy seed after thee; Every man child among you shall be circumcised.
And ye shall circumcise the flesh of your foreskin, and it shall be a token of the covenant betwixt me and you."

-Genesis 17:10-11

God also entered a covenant with Abraham by commanding him to circumcise all the male born in his house including himself and it was supposed to be an ordinance which was to be done for all newborn after eight days. You may not feel the excruciating pain of circumcision while you are young, when the skin is still soft and tender. But undergoing such at an old age is an instruction with excruciating pain. Still, Abraham obeyed.

Part of the blessing attached to this instruction as contained in Genesis 17:9 was that God would give him and his seed the land where they were strangers for an everlasting possession. So Abraham secured this generational blessing on the platform of fulfilling his part of the covenant.

Total obedience to God is an important key that is required to walk into generational blessing, The Bible gives an example of people such as Saul, Eli, Ananias and Sapphira who did not obey God fully, and this made their generation to be cut off from being enlisted among those who enjoyed generational blessing.

CHAPTER SIX

DON'T DROP THE BALL

"God has equipped you to handle difficult things. He has already planted the seeds of blessings inside you. You have to water those seeds with His word to make them grow."

-Joyce Meyer

Generational blessing is free, but not without some conditions to receiving it. Growing the seed of generational blessing to the point of its bearing fruit takes diligence, hard work, self-control, courage, faith, and adequate preparation. Yes, we know that, things that we do not prepare well for are not crucial to our living. But one thing that we must remember is that generational blessing is important to our present and future living. And to help you, all that you need to receive your generational blessing has been provided by God.

In this chapter, I want to show you how to make generational blessing work in your life, for now, and the future.

It is one thing to know what is available for you, but it's more important to understand how to partake from it. It's important to know that every provision of scriptures leave you with responsibility for you to benefit from it. For instance, as free as salvation with all the attendant benefits, if you do not repent, you cannot be saved. We serve a covenant keeping God, so when our part is played, we enjoy the blessing.

> *"For ye have need of patience, that, after ye have done the will of God, ye might receive the promise."*

> **-Hebrews 10:36**

Does it really matter?

People ask: "Does it matter what my parents or God said about me for the future?" I tell you, my friend, it does. There is a power of attorney that the Creator gave to our parents. That power is reflected in their pronouncement, which is made on their offspring. What I mean is that you should be interested in what your father or mother says about your future. Much more, what God says about your today and tomorrow is important.

> *"Honor your father and your mother that your days may be long on the land which the Lord your God gives you."*

-Exodus 20:12

Rebecca, Isaac's wife, knew the power in the pronouncement of a father on his generations to come. **And Esau, the first son of Isaac, will never forget the power in a father's utterance.**

To say that generational blessing does not matter is to say that God's promises are not important. Yet we know this is not true.

Have you noticed that many people see generational curses as more potent than a generational blessing? The question is, why do we believe more in curses than in blessings? I will rather believe more in God's promises and my father's positive pronouncements on me than in curses, which the redemptive power of Christ has taken away.

If we look through the bible, we will observe that there are always laid out strategies accompanying God's promises that becomes instructions on how to obtain those promises. This means in order to obtain that promise, we have a part to play, irrespective of the extent of that part. Some blessings are terminated at some point in a generation when a man does not play his part. The flow of blessing stops where our part of the covenant stops. What then are some of the condition and ways to connect with the promises of generational blessings?

1. Grow the planted seed

Generational blessing is the fruit of a seed that was, at one time in the past, planted by our parents and God. You need to grow the seed; else it will die off and rot. Sometimes, we wonder why God's great promises are not fulfilled or why the positive wishes of parents are not manifest in their children. It is because the seed of generational blessing planted years back are not grown by those who should be the beneficiaries.

This is simple, the seed has been planted by God Himself and your parents. All you need to do is to spot the seed and grow it to maturity.

At this juncture, I want to present a powerful tool for perpetuating and receiving generational blessings. Every parent and child must recognize, use and not abuse words of power and pronouncements of blessings.

Words can Nurture or Destroy Seeds of Greatness

The truth is, words are powerful! I strongly believe it is high time we line our children up and consciously begin to pronounce and declare generational blessings over them.

Let us begin to intentionally and authoritatively speak great and positive things, traits, virtues, habits, lifestyles, skills and possessions over them. I'm talking about those good things that we have previously seen with our parents and generations before us. This is the surest way to keep the blessings rolling! Once again, ***don't drop the ball.***

I have realized that, we sometimes slip into an unhealthy habit of remembering the negative attributes of our parents and those before them, but it's time to stop focusing on that. We need to start acknowledging good things about our ancestry and view their lives from a more positive perspective. There is always something good about people.

This is why, I am sure that there a lot of positive things you can find in your ancestry. So, if you can't find a possession, then find a virtue, honourable lifestyle, good talent or useful skill.

Some of us have in our ancestry a great commitment to work and life just like my mother. Wow! If that is the case, then, I encourage you to hold on to that and speak it over your children and their children too. **_Don't drop the ball!_**

Some have parents, like my father who are very confidential in handling people's affairs. Awesome! I encourage you to hold on to that and speak it over your children and their children too. **_Don't drop the ball!_**

Some have parents (like my mother) who are great with time management skills, business acumen, accounting skills and trade expertise. Awesome! I encourage you to hold on to that and speak it over your children and their children too. **_Don't drop the ball!_**

For some, your parents managed other people's business very well, no matter how insignificant that business was, hold on to that virtue and speak it with authority and power over your own children. ***Don't drop that ball!***

Some saw their parents work for the government, had high integrity, were much respected even when their position seemed void of affluence; yet they remained influential. Hey! If this is the case for your parents, then, I challenge you to hold on to that virtue of integrity and speak it over your children and their children after them. ***Keep the blessings rolling!***

Some of you saw your single parent manage resources like they had everything and everyone on their side, put a finger on that management ability and speak it over your children. You will be ever happy that you intentionally ***didn't drop that ball!***

Intention is key, conscious effort has no short cut! We MUST consciously stop SPEAKING the negative over our lives and our children, no matter the context or constrain!

You will give 'account' of every word you speak, not those you think. **Speak well if you want to live well**; speak blessings forward into your family if you want to see blessings fall on generations after you.

You may say, I'm not sure 1 can do this. My friend, I can relate with how you feel. I understand that, there will be times when it seems like all you think and remember are the negative issues that were laced into your past by your parents and those you trusted.

Your chaotic childhood, abusive parents and distant ancestry may cast an ugly shadow over your mind about positive opportunities of the past that are still potent for the future. You may think there is nothing to glean from those who have gone before you.

Please, think again! I want you to remember and realize that, you inherited your DNA and physical form. They were handed to you by a biological process that didn't start with you. Your mother's womb housed the seed from your father and the outcome is the man or woman standing before the mirror today.

So, even though you have myriads of reasons to be angry and dissatisfied, yet you must also choose to look on the brighter side and be grateful. Your height, skin colour, beautiful eyes, curvy shape, fine hair and agile body are all gifts from God to you, through your parents.

So, why not make every effort to pick and speak positive things from your ancestry. You will be glad you did!

Watch this scenario as an example:

My father is a great man; yet not perfect! I still remember how he managed resources kept in his care in a small village shop. Great news! Today, I am managing resources and will manage resources in mega organisations and enterprise. Emphasis on the word **'MANAGE'**. That is the dominant and active word for this story.

Now notice…My father managed another person's business *astutely*, but I am managing my group of companies *greatly*. God is so faithful! Generational blessings are real! I'm a living proof!

So, speak with every sense of consciousness, intention and duty. This is because, to grow the seed of generational blessing, you need to 'MIND your Language - consciously think, process and speak your words. They have power in them- use and not abuse.

In addition to this, you must:

-Understand that the seed was planted for your sake

I believe that you are already well acquainted with the meaning of generational blessing from the previous chapters of this book. But to be able to receive it, a good understanding is essential. What do I mean? There are specific generational blessings meant for you. Hence, you must pull yourself out of the crowd and know that you are the target of the blessing. This understanding will help you grow the seed of generational blessing to maturity.

-Explore the depth of the seed

Now that you understand that the blessing is for you, you need to explore it. The Word Net dictionary defines the word 'explore' as; "To search through or into; to penetrate or range over for discovery; to examine thoroughly.........." It is your duty to search for God's promises, as revealed in the Bible and your parents' blessings. For example, in Deuteronomy 28:1-13, God pronounced all-encompassing present and future benefits on obedient children. You need to explore them so that you can grow them.

-Receive the blessing, personalize it

To receive the revealed generational blessing is to appropriate it into your personal life. Now, there is a vast difference between a promise for a group, a community, or a church, and you as an individual. When people shout "Amen!" to a said prayer, don't you think that there are some who say so because they are in the pew? They do not believe that the answer to the prayer is for them. Probably they are correct. But there are some who, in reality, believe that the promises are meant for them. To grow the seed of generational blessing, you must receive it as it's meant for you specifically.

Generational blessing can be lost

Frankly, no matter how weighty and powerful generational blessing is, it is wisdom to know that it cannot only be limited, it can also be lost. You need to know that generational blessings are unparalleled lifetime opportunities. They are difficult to recover once lost. When you, as the supposed beneficiary of great generational pronouncements, fail to understand, explore, and receive your generational blessing, you are losing the privilege of enjoying the blessing already.

-The story of Esau

The story Esau is a typical example of loss of generational blessing. If he had understood that his future depended wholly on his father's (Isaac's) pronouncement of generational blessing on him, he would not have despised his birthright. Thus, he lost the right of the first son to his Brother Jacob

-The arrow can be shot more than thrice

Do you know that you can eventually lose your generational blessing by limiting the possibilities through it? An interesting story on this is recorded in 2 Kings13:14 -19. Elisha was sick, and he would soon die. At this time, Jeroboam was the King of Israel, and he was to receive a generational blessing from Elisha, the prophet. Elisha gave him two instructions: hold my hand and shoot the arrow eastward, and to smite the arrow on the ground. The king did shoot the arrow but only smashed the arrow on the ground three times instead of as many as possible. His generational blessing of perpetual victory on the enemy nations was reduced to only three times.

What do I mean? Make good use of the opportunity that the seed of generational blessing provides. Let the seed of your generational blessing grow and have tentacles here and there. Enjoy the blessing to the full because half success is far from excellence.

How to maintain the generational blessing

Do you know that you can receive and maintain your generational blessing all the time? You only need to:

-Put God first

You must recognize and put God first in order to enjoy and maintain your generational blessing. The beginning of enjoying lifelong generational blessing is salvation in Christ. Actually, a blessing without salvation in Christ is the same as generational curses. When you become converted into Christ through faith, even generational curses are turned into a generational blessing.

-Follow the Rechabites' Principle of Obedience

> *"And Jeremiah said unto the house of the Rechabites, Thus said the Lord Of hosts, the God of Israel; because you have obeyed the commandment of Jonadab your father, and kept all his precepts, and done according to all that he has commanded you". Therefore thus said the Lord of hosts, the God of Israel; Jonadab, the son of Rechab shall not want (lack) a man before me forever."*

-Jeremiah 35:18, 19

To continue enjoying the generational blessing pronounced by God and their father, the Rechabites must continue to obey the commandment of not to drink wine.

Sincerely, my friend, there are conditions attached to enjoying generational blessing, one of which is complete obedience to God's laws. You cannot work against the principles of generational blessing and yet seek to enjoy it.

-Act like the Zelophehad Daughters: Pray and Possess

It is pertinent to ask this, is generational blessing gender sensitive? I say no. Zelophehad died without a male child. By virtue of the existing laws in Israel, his daughters would not inherit anything in spite of the promise of generational blessing on them. They had to ask (pray) for what belonged to them, and they got it. Also, being a man or woman does not exclude you from enjoying your generational blessing.

-Work hard, pay the price

Now that you know that you can enjoy the generational blessing, do you sit, fold your arms and wait for the seed to grow? Not at all! The real fact is that, work must be done for the seed of generational blessing to grow into a tree that will benefit you and others around you

CONCLUSION

Anything that you can't take beyond the grave
is not a blessing in the real sense. The only
generational blessing that you take beyond the
grave is Eternal life, and this only can be found
in Christ Jesus. The desire of God is for us to
leave a robust life that goes beyond us. But it's
a pity that this is not the idea of most people,
a typical person is brainwashed to get all he
can, can all he gets and sit on the can, while
depriving future generations from the blessing
that should be continuing. A lot of people
live in a manner that jeopardizes the future
generation. You have a choice to make, either to
be a blessing to the future generation or a curse.
Choose wisely.

Printed in Great Britain
by Amazon

76238818R00057